How to Use Language Central for Math

This book will help you **think, talk,** and **write** about what you are learning in your math class. Every lesson has 4 pages to help you learn the language needed to succeed in math.

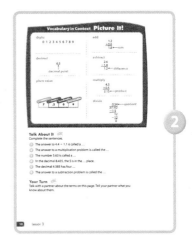

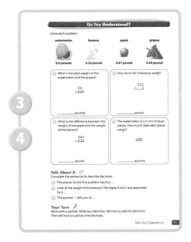

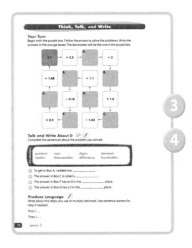

1. Activities connect what you know with what you will learn.
   Look for the **blue bar** on the first page.

2. Vocabulary terms are shown with pictures to help you learn what they mean.
   Look for the **red box** on the second page.

3. Look for clues to help you know when to write an answer and when to speak an answer .

4. Practice the skills you learn in your math class.

CONTENTS
Grade 5

Place Value

Essential Question What vocabulary terms will help you discuss place value and compare numbers?

You Will
- Represent and compare numbers from thousandths to millions.
- Use standard form, word form, and expanded form to write numbers.
- Use math vocabulary to express place-value ideas.

Talk About It

Rate these mathematical terms according to the following scale:

1. I have never heard of this term.
2. I have heard this term, but I do not know how to use it in math.
3. I understand this term and I know how to use it in math.

_____ millions	_____ thousandths
_____ hundred thousands	_____ place value
_____ ten thousands	_____ decimal
_____ thousands	_____ standard form
_____ hundreds	_____ expanded form
_____ tens	_____ word form
_____ ones	_____ digits
_____ tenths	_____ is greater than
_____ hundredths	_____ is less than

Explain what you know about each term, using the sentence starters.

I do not know what … means.
I think … means …
I know … means … in math.

Your Turn

Look at the objectives under You Will at the top of the page. Working with a partner, predict what you are going to learn. Use the sentence starter for support.

I am going to learn about …

digits 0 1 2 3 4 5 6 7 8 9

decimal 21.75

└─decimal point

place value

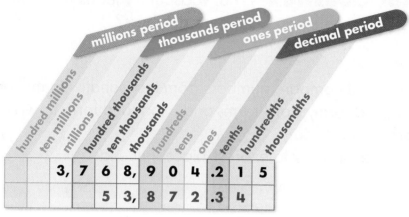

The **value** of the 3 is 3,000.

The **value** of the 4 is 0.04.

standard form 53,872.34

expanded form 50,000 + 3,000 + 800 + 70 + 2 + 0.3 + 0.04

word form fifty-three thousand, eight hundred seventy-two and thirty-four hundredths

compare Tell how things are the same or different.

15 **is greater than** 13.	24 **is less than** 31.	12 + 4 **is equal to** 16.
15 > 13	24 < 31	12 + 4 = 16

Talk About It

Talk with a partner to complete the sentences.

1. In the number 6,120.435, the 5 is in the ... place.

2. The value of the 6 in 6,309,452.178 is ...

3. 150 < 179 means 150 ... 179.

Your Turn

Look at the first number in the place-value chart above. Read the number to a partner. Tell the value of each digit.

Here is some information about elephants and giraffes. Write the green numbers in the place-value chart.

3.6 meters

4.85 meters

About **660,000** elephants in the world

About **150,000** giraffes in the world

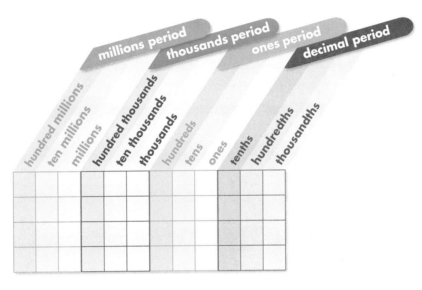

Talk About It

How can you describe these numbers? Complete the sentences.

1. The value of the 6 in 3.6 is …
2. The ones and the tenths places are separated by a …
3. The number 150,000 has a 5 in the … place.
4. The word form for the number of elephants is …
5. The number of elephants … the number of giraffes.

Your Turn

Use at least 4 digits to write a number without a decimal point. Write another number that has at least 4 digits *and* a decimal point. Say the word form of each number to a partner. Then tell the value of each digit.

Think, Talk, and Write

Your Turn

1 Write 1,583,018 in standard form, word form, and expanded form.

Standard Form: _____

Word Form: _____

_____

Expanded Form: _____

_____

2 Write 852.76 in standard form, word form, and expanded form.

Standard Form: _____

Word Form: _____

_____

Expanded Form: _____

3 Compare these numbers. Write >, <, or =.

27,609 _____ 29,540

Talk and Write About It

Complete the sentences about place value and comparing numbers.

Vocabulary			
millions	is greater than	ones	is less than
value	ten thousands	tenths	hundredths
digit	hundred thousands	hundreds	thousandths

4 In 1,583,018, the 5 is in the _____ place.

5 In the number 852.76, the 6 is in the _____ place.

6 In Problem 3, the symbol I wrote means _____ .

Produce Language

Write about how place value helps you read and write numbers. Use as many vocabulary terms as you can. Share with a partner.

Whole-Number Operations

Essential Question What words and symbols should you understand and use when you talk about operations?

You Will
- Add and subtract whole numbers using an algorithm.
- Multiply and divide whole numbers using an algorithm.
- Use math vocabulary to describe addition, subtraction, multiplication, and division.

Talk About It

Copy each term from Vocabulary in Context on a card.
As your teacher reads each term, create three piles of cards.

Pile 1 I know what this term means.
Pile 2 I have heard of this term, but I am not sure how it is used in math.
Pile 3 I have not heard of this term.

What do you know about each term? Explain, using the sentence starters for support.

I know … means …
I think … means …
I do not know what … means.

product

divide

subtraction

Your Turn
Look at the objectives listed under You Will at the top of the page. Working with a partner, predict what you will learn. Use the sentence starter below.

I am going to learn about …

Vocabulary in Context **Picture It!**

whole numbers
2, 8, 17, 104

add

plus — ↓ equals
addition sentence: 8 + 2 = 10
addends   sum

subtract

subtraction sentence: 6 − 2 = 4
minus —
difference

algorithm A step-by-step way to solve a problem

regroup

```
    1
   4 7
 + 3 8        15 ones = 1 ten 5 ones
   8 5
```

multiply

multiplication sentence:
factors
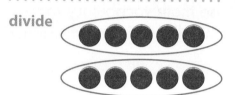
4 × 3 = 12
times —   product

divide
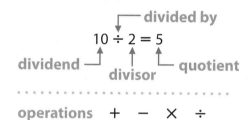

division sentence:
divided by
10 ÷ 2 = 5
dividend —   quotient
divisor

operations + − × ÷

```
 8 12
 9 2         9 tens 2 ones =
 − 1 7       8 tens 12 ones
   7 5
```

Talk About It

Complete the sentences.

1. 25 − 19 = 6 is a ... sentence.

2. When you multiply, the answer is the ...

3. 7, 38, and 210 are all ...

4. When you divide, the answer is called the ...

Your Turn

Choose an operation on this page. Think about what it means to you. Tell a partner.

Complete each problem. Show the steps of each algorithm you use.

1. A garden has 4 rows of plants with 13 plants in each row. How many plants are there in all?

```
  13
× 4
```

There are _____ plants in all.

2.
```
  548
+171
```

3.
```
  632
−315
```

4.
```
3)42
```

Talk About It
Complete the sentences.

5. In Problem 1, the numbers 13 and 4 are called …

6. The answer to Problem 2 is called the …

7. To subtract the ones in Problem 3, first I had to …

8. To solve Problem 4, I had to …

Your Turn
Talk with a partner. Tell what you know about the parts of a division problem. Use the sentence starter below if you need help.

In a division problem, …

Your Turn

For each problem below, choose two numbers from the box to make an addition, subtraction, multiplication, or division problem. Then find the answer. Show all the steps.

> 6 84   **20**   4
>
>   108   105
>   15
> 34   5   18

1 _____ + _____ = _____

2 _____ – _____ = _____

3 _____ × _____ = _____

4 _____)‾‾‾‾‾

Talk and Write About It

Complete the sentences about the problems you solved.

Vocabulary

sum	division	product	difference
quotient	whole numbers	minus	algorithm

5 All the numbers in the box are _____ .

6 The answer to my subtraction problem is called the _____ .

7 The step-by-step way I solve a problem is called an _____ .

8 The answer to my division problem is called the _____ .

Produce Language

Write about the steps you used to solve one of your problems. Use sentence starters for help, if needed.

First, I …

Then, I …

Last, I …

Decimal Operations

Essential Question What vocabulary terms do you need in order to learn about decimals?

You Will
- Add, subtract, multiply, and divide decimals.
- Solve word problems involving decimals.
- Use math vocabulary to talk and write about decimals.

Talk About It

Tear out the School Shopping Four Corners Activity sheet on pages 91–92. Then cut out the activity cards on page 93.

Work with a partner.

You will use the activity cards to solve problems. Each corner of the room tells you how many cards to choose.

Step 1 Place the cards facedown in a pile.

Step 2 Go to a corner of the room. Follow the directions. Choose the correct number of activity cards.

Step 3 Find the box on your activity sheet that matches the corner. Paste the activity card(s) in the box. Then solve the problem written in the box.

Repeat Steps 1, 2, and 3 for each corner of the room.

Look at the red terms in each box. What do you know about these terms? Use the sentence starters for support.

I know … means …
I think … means …
I do not know what … means.

Your Turn

Look at the objectives listed under You Will at the top of the page. Working with a partner, predict what you will learn. Use the sentence starter below.

I am going to learn about …

Vocabulary in Context **Picture It!**

digits

0 1 2 3 4 5 6 7 8 9

decimal

6.5

↑
decimal point

place value

ones	tenths	hundredths	thousandths
7	.2	0	9

add

$$
\begin{array}{r}
1.2 \\
+0.6 \\
\hline
1.8
\end{array}
$$
←—sum

subtract

$$
\begin{array}{r}
2.6 \\
-1.4 \\
\hline
1.2
\end{array}
$$
←—difference

multiply

$$
\begin{array}{r}
4.3 \\
\times 0.5 \\
\hline
2.15
\end{array}
$$
←—product

divide

```
        0.54  ←—quotient
    3)1.62
      −1 5
         12
        −12
          0
```

Talk About It

Complete the sentences.

1. The answer to 4.4 ÷ 1.1 is called a …
2. The answer to a multiplication problem is called the …
3. The number 5.63 is called a …
4. In the decimal 8.435, the 5 is in the … place.
5. The decimal 4.385 has four …
6. The answer to a subtraction problem is called the …

Your Turn

Talk with a partner about the terms on this page. Tell your partner what you know about them.

Solve each problem.

watermelon	banana	apple	grapes
9.6 pounds	**0.32 pound**	**0.67 pound**	**0.44 pound**

1 What is the total weight of the watermelon and the grapes?

$$9.6$$
$$+\,0.44$$

_____ pounds

2 How much do 3 bananas weigh?

$$0.32$$
$$\times\quad 3$$

_____ pound

3 What is the difference between the weight of the apple and the weight of the banana?

$$0.67$$
$$-\,0.32$$

_____ pound

4 The watermelon is cut into 4 equal pieces. How much does each piece weigh?

$$4\overline{)9.6}$$

_____ pounds

Talk About It

Complete the sentences to describe decimals.

5 The answer to the first problem has four …

6 Look at the weight of the banana. The digits 0 and 3 are separated by a …

7 The symbol ÷ tells you to …

Your Turn

Work with a partner. Write two decimals. Tell how to add the decimals. Then tell how to subtract the decimals.

Think, Talk, and Write

Your Turn

Begin with the purple box. Follow the arrows to solve the problems. Write the answers in the orange boxes. The last answer will be the one in the purple box.

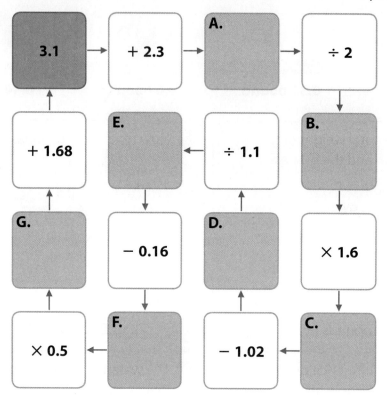

Talk and Write About It

Complete the sentences about the problem you solved.

Vocabulary

product	sum	digits	decimals
tenths	thousandths	difference	hundredths

1. To get to Box A, I added two _____ .

2. The answer in Box C is called a _____ .

3. The answer in Box F has an 8 in the _____ place.

4. The answer in Box G has a 2 in the _____ place.

Produce Language

Write about the steps you use to multiply decimals. Use sentence starters for help if needed.

First, I …

Then, I …

Estimation

Essential Question What do you need to know to understand and discuss estimation?

You Will
- Understand rounding numbers.
- Estimate when computing with numbers.
- Use math vocabulary for estimating.

Talk About It

Look at the list of terms below. In the first two columns of the chart, write terms you **know** or **want** to know more about.

nearest   exactly   estimate
reasonable   about   unreasonable
round

Know	Want	Learned

Tell what you know about each term you wrote in the chart. Use the sentence starters for help.

I know the term …
I think … means …

Your Turn

Look at the objectives listed under You Will at the top of the page. Working with a partner, predict what you are going to learn. Use the sentence starter below to help you.

I am going to learn about …

exactly 287 marbles
about 300 marbles

reasonable guess: 600 marbles
unreasonable guess: 6,000 marbles

round Replace one number with another number that is about the same value.

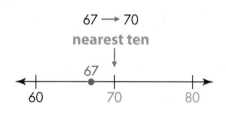

67 → 70
nearest ten

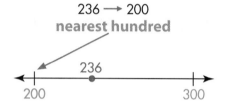

236 → 200
nearest hundred

estimate Tell about how much.

An **estimate** is a logical guess.

Talk About It

Talk with a partner. Complete the sentences.

1. There are ... 7 days in one week.
2. There are ... 500 trees in the park.
3. A logical guess is an ...
4. An estimate of 1,000 pages for my math book is ...

Your Turn

Think of how you would describe the vocabulary terms. Write and/or draw to show what those terms mean to you.

A truck driver travels Route W and Route Z. About how many miles is that?

You can round to the nearest ten to estimate the answer.

Route	Number of Miles
Route W	33
Route X	26
Route Y	18
Route Z	41

33 + 41

↓   ↓

30 + 40 = 70

The distance is about 70 miles.

1 The driver travels Route X and Route Y. About how many miles is that?   about _____ miles

2 For 12 days, the driver travels Route Y each day. About how many miles is that?   about _____ miles

3 The driver uses 2 gallons of gas to travel Route Z. About how many miles does the driver travel on 1 gallon of gas?   about _____ miles

Talk About It

What terms can you use to estimate? Complete the sentences to explain.

4 My answer to Problem 1 is a ... estimate.

5 The number of miles for Route X is ... 26.

6 Route Z is ... 40 miles long.

Your Turn

Round the miles for Route Y and Route Z to the nearest ten. Subtract to estimate the difference between the two routes. Explain to your partner how you found your answer.

Your Turn

Sam's family takes car trips to visit relatives. They come home between visits. Round the number of miles to the nearest hundred to find each estimate.

Person	Number of Miles (round trip)
Grandma	312
Aunt Pat	124
Uncle Bob	188

1 Sam's family visited Grandma and Uncle Bob. About how many miles did they drive?

about _____ miles

2 About how many more miles is a visit to Grandma's than a visit to Aunt Pat's?

about _____ more miles

Talk and Write About It

Complete the sentences about estimation.

<table>
<tr><td rowspan="2">Vocabulary</td></tr>
</table>

nearest ten	round	exactly	estimate
reasonable	nearest hundred	about	unreasonable

3 A visit to Grandma is _____ 300 miles.

4 A visit to Aunt Pat is _____ 124 miles.

5 An estimate of 800 miles for two visits to Uncle Bob is _____ .

Produce Language

Write the terms you learned about in this lesson in the third column of the chart on page 13. Write what you know about these terms. Use sentence starters from throughout the lesson for support.

Simplifying Fractions

Essential Question What vocabulary terms will help you understand fractions and how to simplify them?

You Will
- Understand equivalent fractions.
- Simplify fractions.
- Use math vocabulary to discuss simplifying fractions.

Talk About It

Copy each term from Vocabulary in Context on a card.
As your teacher reads each term, make three piles of cards.

Pile 1 I know what this term means.

Pile 2 I have heard of this term, but I am not sure how it is used in math.

Pile 3 I have not heard of this term.

What do you know about each term? Explain, using the sentence starters for support.

I know … means …
I think … means …
I do not know what … means.

fraction

numerator

simplify

Your Turn
Look at the objectives listed under You Will at the top of the page. Working with a partner, predict what you are going to learn. Use the sentence starter below to help you.

I am going to learn about …

Vocabulary in Context **Picture It!**

fraction

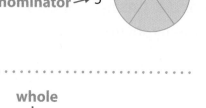

numerator ⟶ $\dfrac{3}{5}$
denominator ⟶

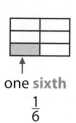 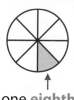

one **sixth**
$\dfrac{1}{6}$

one **eighth**
$\dfrac{1}{8}$

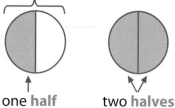

whole

one **half**
$\dfrac{1}{2}$

two **halves**
$\dfrac{2}{2}$

equivalent

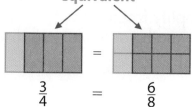

$\dfrac{3}{4}$ = $\dfrac{6}{8}$

one **third**
$\dfrac{1}{3}$

one **fourth**
$\dfrac{1}{4}$

one **fifth**
$\dfrac{1}{5}$

simplify a fraction

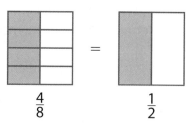

$\dfrac{4}{8}$ = $\dfrac{1}{2}$

$\dfrac{4}{8} = \dfrac{1}{2}$ ÷ 4

4 is the **greatest common factor.**

Talk About It

Talk with a partner. Complete the sentences.

1. The top number in a fraction is the …

2. The bottom number in a fraction is the …

3. $\dfrac{2}{3}$ and $\dfrac{4}{6}$ are …

4. I can simplify a fraction by dividing the numerator and denominator by the …

Your Turn

Tell a partner as many things as you know about $\dfrac{2}{8}$ and $\dfrac{1}{4}$.

Use as many vocabulary terms as possible.

1. Write the missing words and numbers to describe each fraction of a pizza.

   =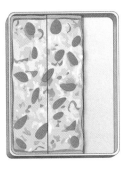

four _____   =   two _____

$\dfrac{\square}{\square}$ = $\dfrac{\square}{\square}$

Simplify the following fractions.

2.

$\dfrac{3}{6}$ = $\dfrac{\square}{\square}$

3.

$\dfrac{6}{8}$ = $\dfrac{\square}{\square}$

Talk About It
Talk about fractions by completing the sentences.

4. When you divide the numerator and denominator of a fraction by the greatest common factor, you … the fraction.

5. A whole with five equal parts is divided into …

6. $\dfrac{8}{8}$ is the same as one …

7. Fractions that describe the same amount are …

Your Turn
Use vocabulary words to explain to your partner how you found the answer in Problem 3.

Think, Talk, and Write

Your Turn

Simplify $\frac{8}{10}$.

Step 1 Find the greatest common factor of the numerator and denominator.

Factors of 8: **1, 2**, 4, and 8
Factors of 10: **1, 2**, 5, and 10
The common factors of 8 and 10 are 1 and 2.
The greatest common factor is 2.

Step 2 Divide the numerator and denominator by the greatest common factor.

$$\frac{8}{10} \div \frac{2}{2} = \frac{4}{5}$$

Step 3 Write the simplified fraction.

$$\frac{4}{5}$$

Simplify the following fractions.

1 $\frac{9}{12} = $ _____

2 $\frac{6}{9} = $ _____

3 $\frac{10}{20} = $ _____

Talk and Write About It

Complete each sentence about simplifying fractions.

Vocabulary		
half	denominator	equivalent
greatest common factor	simplify	numerator

4 The 3 in $\frac{3}{6}$ is called the _____ .

5 After you simply a fraction, the new fraction is _____ to the one you started with.

Produce Language

Write about how to simplify a fraction. You may include an example and drawings. Use as many vocabulary terms as you can. Share with a partner.

Fractions, Decimals, and Percents

Essential Question How can you use vocabulary terms to talk about fractions, decimals, and percents?

You Will
- Identify fractions, decimals, and percents.
- Understand how fractions, decimals, and percents are related.
- Use math vocabulary to talk about fractions, decimals, and percents.

Talk About It

Work with a partner. Make an index card for each vocabulary term below. Place each card in one of three piles.

Pile 1 I know what this term means.
Pile 2 I have heard of this term, but I am not sure how it is used in math.
Pile 3 I have not heard of this term.

percent   convert   part
fraction   equivalent   whole
numerator   denominator   decimal point
decimal

percent

What do you know about each term? Explain, using the sentence starters for support.

I know … means …
I think … means …
I do not know what … means.

Your Turn
Look at the objectives listed under You Will at the top of the page. Working with a partner, predict what you are going to learn. Use the sentence starter below.

I am going to learn about …

Vocabulary in Context **Picture It!**

whole

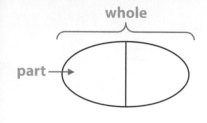

part →

decimal

0.75

↑

decimal point

percent Part per 100

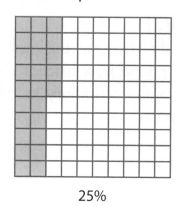

25%

fraction

numerator →
denominator → $\frac{3}{5}$

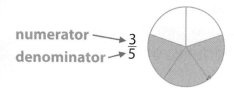

convert Change a number to a different form.

$$50\% = 0.5 = \frac{5}{10}$$

equivalent

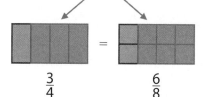

$\frac{3}{4}$ = $\frac{6}{8}$

Talk About It

Talk with a partner. Complete the sentences.

1. 60% is a …

2. The top number in a fraction is the …

3. 50% and $\frac{1}{2}$ are …

Your Turn

Write these numbers: $\frac{4}{10}$, 40%, 0.4. Describe these numbers to a partner. Use as many vocabulary terms as possible.

Look at the quilt pictured below. Write about the pink squares. Write the fraction, decimal, and percent for the pink squares. Use the numbers for the orange squares as a model.

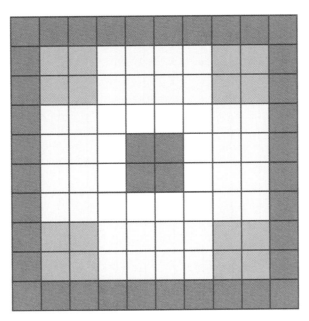

Orange   **Pink**

16 of the 100 squares are orange.

$\frac{16}{100}$, or $\frac{4}{25}$, of the quilt is orange.

0.16 of the quilt is orange.

16% of the quilt is orange.

Talk About It
Complete the sentences to tell about fractions, decimals, and percents.

1. Fractions, decimals, and percents show parts of a ...

2. $\frac{12}{100}$ is the ... of the quilt that is white.

3. 64% equals a fraction with numerator 64 and ... 100.

4. $\frac{16}{100}$, 0.16, and 16% are all ...

Your Turn
Write a few sentences that describe fractions, decimals, and percents. Use the definitions on page 22 for support.

Fractions, Decimals, and Percents   **23**

Your Turn

Draw a quilt with red, blue, and green squares. Use fractions, decimals, and percents to describe the part of the quilt that is made up of each color.

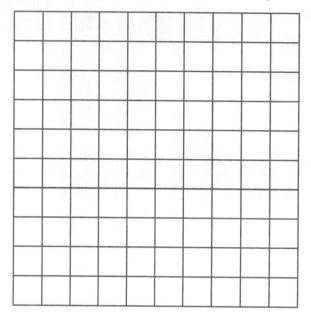

Red   **Blue**   **Green**

Talk and Write About It

Complete the sentences about the quilt you drew.

Vocabulary			
whole	part	percent	numerator
equivalent	decimal	fraction	convert

1 There are 100 squares in the _____ quilt.

2 Red squares make up _____ of the quilt.

3 When I wanted to change a fraction to another form, I needed to _____ it.

Produce Language

Write about how fractions, decimals, and percents are related. You may include examples. Use as many vocabulary words as you can.

Comparing and Ordering Fractions and Decimals

Essential Question How do you use words and symbols (<, >, =) to compare and order fractions and decimals?

You Will

- Use the symbols >, <, and = to compare and order fractions and decimals.
- Use math vocabulary to compare and order fractions and decimals.

Talk About It

Rate these mathematical terms according to the following scale.

1. I do not know this term.

2. I have heard this term, but I do not know how to use it in math.

3. I understand this term and I know how to use it in math.

_____ point   _____ is greater than (>)
_____ number line   _____ mixed number
_____ is less than (<)   _____ is equal to (=)
_____ least to greatest   _____ greatest to least
_____ symbols   _____ order

Explain what you know about each term, using the sentence starters.

I do not know what ... means.
I think ... means ...
I know ... means ... in math.

Your Turn

Look at the objectives under You Will at the top of the page. Working with a partner, predict what you are going to learn. Use the sentence starter for support.

I am going to learn about ...

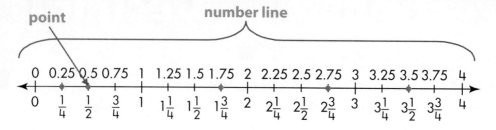

point   number line

0   0.25 0.5 0.75   1   1.25 1.5 1.75   2   2.25 2.5 2.75   3   3.25 3.5 3.75   4

0   $\frac{1}{4}$ $\frac{1}{2}$ $\frac{3}{4}$ 1 $1\frac{1}{4}$ $1\frac{1}{2}$ $1\frac{3}{4}$ 2 $2\frac{1}{4}$ $2\frac{1}{2}$ $2\frac{3}{4}$ 3 $3\frac{1}{4}$ $3\frac{1}{2}$ $3\frac{3}{4}$ 4

0.25 is less than $\frac{1}{2}$ 1.75 is equal to $1\frac{3}{4}$ 3.5 is greater than $2\frac{3}{4}$

$0.25 < \frac{1}{2}$ (equals)

$1.75 = 1\frac{3}{4}$ $3.5 > 2\frac{3}{4}$

mixed number

order

least to greatest
10, 17, 128

greatest to least
128, 17, 10

symbols

>   <   =

Talk About It

Talk with a partner to complete these sentences.

1. 2.5 > 0.75 means two and five tenths … seventy-five hundredths.
2. $2\frac{1}{4}$ … 2.25.
3. $3\frac{1}{4}$ is a …
4. $\frac{1}{4}$ … 0.75.
5. 2.25 … $1\frac{1}{2}$.

Your Turn

Tell a partner what you know about the terms and symbols on this page.

The distances three grasshoppers jumped are shown below.

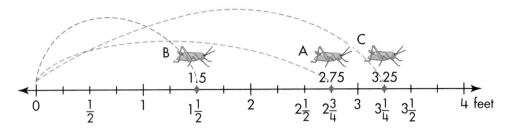

Grasshopper A jumped 2.75 feet. Grasshopper B jumped 1.5 feet.
To compare these distances, you can write:

$$2.75 > 1.5 \text{ or } 1.5 < 2.75$$

1 Write Grasshopper C's distance as a decimal. _____

Write Grasshopper B's distance as a decimal. _____

Compare the distances. _____

2 Write Grasshopper A's distance as a mixed number _____

Write the Grasshopper C's distance as a mixed number. _____

Compare the distances. _____

3 Write one grasshopper's distance as a decimal. _____

Write another grasshopper's distance as a fraction. _____

Compare the distances. _____

Talk About It

What words and symbols can you use to compare and order numbers?
Complete the sentences to explain.

4 The symbol $>$ means …

5 The symbol $<$ means …

6 The symbol $=$ means …

Your Turn

Choose the distance one grasshopper jumped. Compare this number
to $2\frac{1}{2}$ and 0.75. Write the three numbers in order from least to greatest.

Think, Talk, and Write

Your Turn

Samira ran $4\frac{1}{4}$ miles. John ran 3.75 miles. Estelle ran $5\frac{1}{2}$ miles. Draw a point at each of these numbers. Write the number and the runner's name near each point.

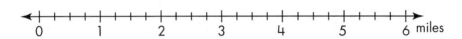

1. The distance Samira ran _____ the distance John ran.

2. The distance Estelle ran _____ the distance Samira ran.

3. The distance Samira ran _____ the distance Estelle ran.

4. Write the distances in order from greatest to least. _____

Talk and Write About It

Complete each sentence about comparing and ordering numbers.

> **Vocabulary**
>
> is greater than (>)   is equal to (=)   is less than (<)   point
> least to greatest   greatest to least   order   symbols

5. If two numbers are the same, use the symbol _____ .

6. If the first number is greater than the second number, use the

   symbol _____ .

7. If you write numbers in order with the biggest one first, they are

   listed from _____ .

Produce Language

Write what you have learned about comparing and ordering numbers. You may use examples. Include as many vocabulary terms and symbols as you can.

Prime and Composite Numbers

Essential Question What vocabulary terms will help you explain prime and composite numbers?

You Will

- Identify prime and composite numbers.
- Use factor trees to break down composite numbers into prime factors.
- Use math vocabulary to explain prime and composite numbers.

Talk About It

Look at the list of terms below. In the first two columns of the chart, write terms you **know** or **want** to know more about.

multiple	factor tree	prime number
factor	composite number	divisible
factor pair	prime factor	

Know	Want	Learned

Tell what you know about each term.

I know the term …
I want to learn …

Your Turn

Look at the objectives under You Will at the top of the page. Working with a partner, predict what you are going to learn. Use the sentence starter for support.

I am going to learn about …

Vocabulary in Context **Picture It!**

multiples of 4

4, 8, 12, 16, …

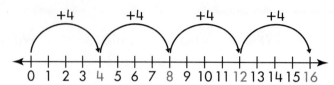

4, 8, 12, 16 are **divisible** by 4.

factors of 24

1, 2, 3, 4, 6, 8, 12, 24

factor pairs for 24

1 × 24   **2 × 12   3 × 8**   4 × 6

A **prime number** has exactly two factors, 1 and itself.
5 is a prime number.

A **composite number** has more than two factors.
6 is a composite number.

factor tree for 24

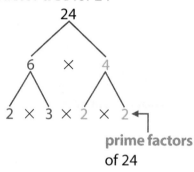

prime factors of 24

Talk About It

Talk with a partner. Complete the sentences.

1. The numbers 5, 10, and 15 are … by 5.
2. The number 8 is a … of 32.
3. The numbers 2, 3, 5, 7, and 11 are …
4. I can use a factor tree to find a number's …
5. There is only one … for a prime number.
6. The number 12 is a …

Your Turn

Write a 2-digit number smaller than 40. Use an many vocabulary terms as you can to describe your number to a partner.

There are 30 chairs in a classroom. They are placed in 6 rows. There are 5 chairs in each row.

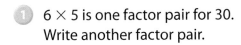

1 6 × 5 is one factor pair for 30. Write another factor pair.

_____

2 Does 30 have more than 2 factors? _____ Is 30 a prime number or a composite

number? _____

3 Use the number of chairs in each row to skip count by 5s. Write down the multiples of 5.

$\underline{\quad5\quad}$, _____ , _____ , _____ , _____ , _____

4 Use the factor tree below. Find the prime factors of 30.

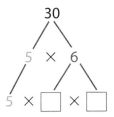

5 What are the prime factors of 30?

_____

Talk About It

What words can you use to talk about prime and composite numbers? Complete the sentences to explain.

6 The numbers 10 and 3 are a ... for 30.

7 A number that has only two factors is a ...

8 The numbers 7, 14, 21, and 28 are ... of 7.

Your Turn

Choose a number from the box. Make a factor tree. Tell your partner whether the number is prime or composite. Explain how you know.

13	20	17
19	22	31

Think, Talk, and Write

Your Turn

In the space below, draw a plan for planting 28 trees. Place trees in more than one row. Put the same number of trees in each row. Then draw a factor tree for 28.

1. How many rows of trees are in your plan? _____

2. How many trees are in each row? _____

3. What factor pair is represented by your plan? _____

   What is another factor pair for 28? _____

4. Is 28 a prime or a composite number? _____ .

5. What are the prime factors of 28? _____ .

6. Is 29 prime or composite? _____ .

Talk and Write About It

Complete each sentence about prime and composite numbers.

Vocabulary			
multiples	factor pair	composite numbers	prime numbers
factors	factor tree	prime factors	divisible

7. 35 is _____ by 5.

8. The numbers 1, 2, 4, 8, 16, and 32 are _____ of 32.

9. The numbers 2, 3, 5, 7, and 11 are _____ .

10. A diagram that helps you find the prime factors of a number is a

    _____ .

11. The numbers 2 and 5 are the only _____ of 10.

Produce Language

Write the terms you learned about in this lesson in the third column of the chart on page 29. Write what you have learned about these terms.

Greatest Common Factor and Least Common Multiple

Essential Question How can you use vocabulary terms to discuss greatest common factor and least common multiple?

You Will

- Find the greatest common factor and least common multiple of two or more numbers.
- Use math vocabulary to discuss greatest common factor and least common multiple.

Talk About It

Make an index card for each vocabulary term below. Place each card in one of three piles.

Pile 1 I know what this term means.
Pile 2 I have heard of this term, but I am not sure how it is used in math.
Pile 3 I have not heard of this term.

common factor

prime number	greatest common factor (GCF)
composite number	common multiple
common factor	least common multiple (LCM)

What do you know about each term? Explain, using the sentence starters for support.

I know … means …
I think … means …
I do not know what … means.

Your Turn

Look at the objectives under You Will at the top of the page. Working with a partner, predict what you are going to learn. Use the sentence starter for support.

I am going to learn about …

Vocabulary in Context **Picture It!**

A **composite number** has more than two factors.
6 is a composite number.

. . . .

A **prime number** has exactly two factors, 1 and itself.
5 is a prime number.

. . . .

common multiples

multiples of 3: 3, 6, 9, 12, 15, 18, 21, 24, 27, 30, 33, 36, …

multiples of 4: 4, 8, 12, 16, 20, 24, 28, 32, 36, 40, …

least common multiple (LCM)

. . . .

common factors

factors of 18: 1, 2, 3, 6, 9, 18

factors of 45: 1, 3, 5, 9, 15, 45

greatest common factor (GCF)

Talk About It
Talk with a partner. Complete the sentences.

1 The smallest multiple that two numbers share is the … of those numbers.

2 The numbers 5 and 13 are …

3 The largest factor that two numbers share is the … of those numbers.

4 A number with more than two factors is a …

Your Turn
Choose two different numbers from 1–9. Use vocabulary terms to describe the numbers to a partner. Then find the least common multiple. Explain your work to a partner.

Do You Understand?

1 Find the greatest common factor (GCF) to solve this problem:

Jasmine has a 12-foot board and a 16-foot board. She wants to cut the boards into pieces that are all the same length. What is the longest she can cut those pieces?

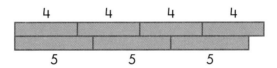

12 feet   16 feet

Factors of 12: _____, _____, _____, _____, _____, _____

Factors of 16: _____, _____, _____, _____, _____

Common factors of 12 and 16: _____, _____, _____

Greatest common factor of 12 and 16: _____

The longest the pieces can be is _____ feet.

2 Find the least common multiple (LCM) to solve this problem:

Look at the brick pattern. The top row is made of 4-inch bricks. The bottom row is made of 5-inch bricks. At how many inches will both rows line up?

4   4   4   4

5   5   5

First ten multiples of 4: _____, _____, _____, _____,

_____, _____, _____, _____, _____, _____

First eight multiples of 5: _____, _____, _____, _____,

_____, _____, _____, _____

Two common multiples of 4 and 5: _____ and _____

Least common multiple of 4 and 5: _____

The bricks will line up at _____ inches.

Talk About It
Complete the sentences.

3 The largest factor that two numbers share is the …

4 The smallest multiple that two numbers share is the …

Your Turn
Choose two numbers from the box. Write the factors and some multiples of each number. Tell your partner about the greatest common factor and least common multiple of both numbers.

| 4 | 5 | 8 |
| 6 | 9 | 10 |

Greatest Common Factor and Least Common Multiple   35

Your Turn

Suppose you use the blue, red, and yellow blocks to make a wall. The wall will have yellow blocks in the bottom row, red blocks in the middle row, and blue blocks in the top row. The wall is finished the first time all of the rows line up. Draw the wall on the grid. The first yellow block is drawn for you.

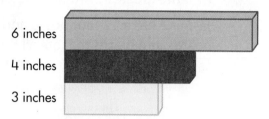

6 inches

4 inches

3 inches

1. How many blue blocks are in the wall? _____

2. How many red blocks are in the wall? _____

3. How many yellow blocks are in the wall? _____

4. What is the least common multiple of 6, 4, and 3? _____

5. How long is the wall? _____

Talk and Write About It

Complete each sentence.

Vocabulary

common multiples	prime numbers
least common multiple (LCM)	common factors
greatest common factor (GCF)	composite numbers

6. The number 6 is the _____ of 24 and 30.

7. The numbers 4, 6, and 21 are _____ .

8. The numbers 6, 12, and 18 are _____ of 2 and 3.

Produce Language

Write about how to find the greatest common factor and least common multiple of two numbers. Use as many vocabulary terms as you can. Share with a partner.

Fraction Operations

Essential Question What words and symbols should you use when you talk about fraction operations?

You Will

- Add, subtract, multiply, and divide fractions.
- Use math vocabulary to describe addition, subtraction, multiplication, and division of fractions.

Talk About It

Copy each term from Vocabulary in Context on a card. As your teacher reads each term, create three piles of cards.

1. Place terms that you know in **Pile 1.**
2. Place terms you have heard but are not sure what they mean in **Pile 2.**
3. Place terms you do not know in **Pile 3.**

What do you know about each term? Explain, using the sentence starters for support.

I know … means …
I think … means …
I do not know what … means.

common denominator

mixed number

reciprocal

Your Turn

Look at the objectives listed under You Will at the top of the page. Working with a partner, predict what you are going to learn. Use the sentence starter for support.

I am going to learn about …

Vocabulary in Context **Picture It!**

improper fraction

$$\frac{7}{4} \qquad \frac{4}{4}$$

mixed number

$$3\frac{5}{6} \qquad 1\frac{1}{2}$$

reciprocals

$$\frac{3}{10} \diagdown \diagup \frac{10}{3}$$

equivalent fractions

$$\frac{3}{4} \qquad = \qquad \frac{6}{8}$$

least common multiple (LCM)

multiples of 4: 4, 8, 12
multiples of 6: 6, 12, 18

$$\frac{1}{3} \qquad \frac{2}{3}$$

**common denominator
(like denominator)**

$$\frac{2}{3} \qquad \frac{1}{2}$$

unlike denominators

$$\frac{2}{3} = \frac{4}{6}$$

$$\frac{1}{2} = \frac{3}{6}$$

**least common
denominator (LCD)**

Talk About It

Talk with a partner. Complete the sentences.

1. Fractions with different denominators have …

2. A number that is made up of a whole number and a fraction is a …

3. A fraction with a numerator that is greater than or equal to the denominator is an …

Your Turn ✏️

Choose a term on this page. Write what it means to you. Share with a partner. Use the sentence starter for help.

I think … means …

Do You Understand?

1 Mr. Bennett bought two pieces of cloth. One piece is $\frac{1}{3}$ yard and the other is $\frac{1}{4}$ yard. How much cloth did he buy?

_____ yard

1

$\frac{1}{3}$	$\frac{1}{4}$

$\frac{1}{12}$	$\frac{1}{12}$	$\frac{1}{12}$	$\frac{1}{12}$	$\frac{1}{12}$	$\frac{1}{12}$	$\frac{1}{12}$

2 Complete these examples of fraction operations.

Fraction Addition and Subtraction

- Find the least common denominator.
- Rewrite the fractions.
- Add or subtract the numerators.
- Keep the same denominator.

$$\frac{3}{4} - \frac{1}{3} = \frac{9}{12} - \frac{4}{12} = \frac{\boxed{}}{12}$$

Fraction Multiplication

- Multiply the numerators.
- Multiply the denominators.

$$\frac{4}{5} \times \frac{2}{3} = \frac{\boxed{}}{\boxed{}}$$

Fraction Division

- Change the second fraction to its reciprocal.
- Change ÷ to × and multiply.

$$2 \div \frac{1}{4} = \frac{2}{1} \times \frac{4}{1} = \frac{\boxed{}}{\boxed{}} = \boxed{}$$

Talk About It

Complete the sentences.

3 The fractions $\frac{1}{3}$ and $\frac{4}{12}$ are …

4 To add or subtract fractions, first find the …

Your Turn

Talk with a partner. Share what you know about dividing fractions.

Think, Talk, and Write

Your Turn

Choose numbers from the box. Use the numbers to write your own problems using addition, subtraction, multiplication, and division. Solve your problems. Be sure to show your work.

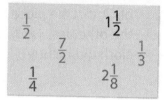

addition sentence:

_____ + _____ = _____

subtraction sentence:

_____ − _____ = _____

multiplication sentence:

_____ × _____ = _____

division sentence:

5 ÷ _____ = _____

Talk and Write About It

Complete the sentences about the fractions in the box.

Vocabulary

reciprocals	like denominators
mixed number	least common multiple
improper fraction	unlike denominators

1. The denominators of $\frac{7}{2}$ and $\frac{1}{2}$ are _____ .

2. $2\frac{1}{8}$ is a _____ .

3. The denominators of $\frac{1}{4}$ and $\frac{1}{3}$ are _____ .

Produce Language

Write about the steps you used to solve one of your problems. Use sentence starters for help if needed.

I know how to solve …
First, I …
Then, I …
Last, I …

Ratios

Essential Question How can you use vocabulary terms to talk about ratios?

You Will
- Use data and models to find ratios.
- Multiply and divide to make equal ratios.
- Use math vocabulary to talk and write about ratios.

Talk About It

Rate these mathematical terms according to the following scale.

1. I do not know this term.

2. I have heard this term, but I do not know how to use it in math.

3. I understand this term and I know how to use it in math.

_____ ratio	_____ table
_____ equal ratios	_____ data
_____ symbol	_____ data set
_____ simplify	

Explain what you know about each term, using the sentence starters.

I do not know what ... means.
I think ... means ...
I know ... means ... in math.

Your Turn
Look at the objectives under You Will at the top of the page. Working with a partner, predict what you are going to learn. Use the sentence starter for support.

I am going to learn about ...

Vocabulary in Context **Picture It!**

A **ratio** of apples to bananas

4 to 6   4 : 6 $\frac{4}{6}$

equal ratios

2 : 6   =   4 : 12

table

Dollars	Quarters
1	4
2	8
3	12
4	16
5	20

data   Collected information

Math Scores

85, 90, 83, 94, 80

data set

simplify a ratio

$\frac{2}{4}$ = $\frac{1}{2}$

2:4   =   1:2

Talk About It

Talk with a partner. Complete the sentences.

1   A group of information is called a …

2   $9 : 5$, $\frac{9}{5}$, and 9 to 5 are three different ways to write a …

3   $2 : 4$ and $3 : 6$ are …

Your Turn

Write and/or draw what you know about the terms on this page. Tell your partner what you know about them.

Each time Dan's cat, Tabby, eats 1 bowl of cat food, his dog, Wags, eats 2 bowls of dog food. Complete the table.

Bowls of Food Dan's Pets Eat	
Tabby	**Wags**
1	2
2	4
3	
4	
5	
6	
7	

Use the table to write three equal ratios that compare the number of bowls of cat food to the number of bowls of dog food.

$$\frac{\quad}{\quad} = \frac{\quad}{\quad} = \frac{\quad}{\quad}$$

Talk About It

What terms can you use to talk about ratios? Complete the sentences to explain.

1. Collected information is called …

2. 2 : 3 is the same as 4 : 6 because they are …

3. You change 6 : 12 to 1 : 2 when you …

Your Turn

Look back at the three ratios you wrote about bowls of pet food. Write to explain how you know the three ratios are equal. Use vocabulary terms. Share your answer with a partner.

Think, Talk, and Write

Your Turn

Look at the basketballs and tennis balls on each shelf.

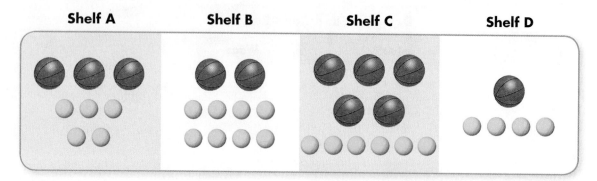

Shelf A **Shelf B** **Shelf C** **Shelf D**

1. What is the ratio of basketballs to tennis balls for Shelf A? _____ : _____

2. What is the ratio of basketballs to tennis balls for Shelf B? _____ : _____

3. What is the ratio of basketballs to tennis balls for Shelf C? _____ : _____

4. What is the ratio of basketballs to tennis balls for Shelf D? _____ : _____

5. Which two shelves have the an equal ratio of basketballs to tennis balls?

   _____

Talk and Write About It

Complete each sentence.

Vocabulary		
ratio	simplify	data
equal ratios	table	data set

6. When you write a fraction or ratio with smaller numbers, you

   _____ it.

7. 3:5 and 6:10 are _____ .

8. Information that is collected is called _____ .

Produce Language

Write about how you can simplify equal ratios to compare them. Use as many vocabulary terms as you can. Share with a partner.

Variables

Essential Question What words do you need to know to discuss variables?

You Will
- Identify variables.
- Write algebraic expressions.
- Use math vocabulary to discuss variables.

Talk About It

Look at the list of terms below. In the first two columns of the chart, write terms you **know** or **want** to know more about.

variable	algebraic equation	missing number	inverse operations
expression	equals	solve	represents
equation	algebraic expression	solution	value

Know	Want	Learned

Tell what you know about each term.

I know the term …
I want to learn …

Your Turn

Look at the objectives under You Will at the top of the page. Working with a partner, predict what you are going to learn. Use the sentence starter for support.

I am going to learn about …

Vocabulary in Context Picture It!

expression
$$7 + 4$$

equation
$$7 + 4 = 11$$
equals

variable

$$6 + c \qquad \boxed{} \div 3 = 4$$

A variable **represents** a **missing number.**

algebraic expression
$$7 + k$$

algebraic equation
$$11 - \triangle = 7$$

inverse operations

+ and −	× and ÷
$10 + 8 = 18$	$5 \times 7 = 35$
$18 - 8 = 10$	$35 \div 7 = 5$

Solve Find the **value** of the variable.
$$\boxed{} + 32 = 40$$
$$\boxed{} = 8 \longleftarrow \text{solution}$$

Talk About It

Talk with a partner. Complete the sentences.

1. The $\triangle$ in $5 + \triangle$ is a …
2. $8 - 3$ is an …
3. $=$ means …
4. $8 \times b$ is an …
5. $15 \div 3 = 5$ is an …
6. Multiplication and division are …

Your Turn

Think about the new vocabulary terms.

- Write an algebraic equation. Use a as the variable.
- Have your partner solve your equation.
- Use vocabulary terms to discuss your partner's work.

Do You Understand?

Use variables to solve the problems.

1. Each box holds the same number of golf balls. How many balls are in each box?

72 golf balls in all

The algebraic expression for all of the golf balls is $6 \times \triangle$.

The algebraic equation is $6 \times \triangle = 72$.

The value of $\triangle$ is _____ .

Each box holds _____ golf balls.

2. How many flying discs are in the barrel?

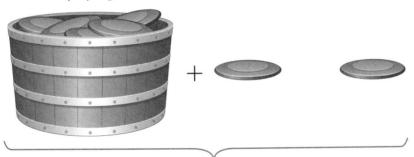

$+$

A total of 85 flying discs

Suppose d represents the number of disks in the barrel. The algebraic

expression for all of the discs is _____ .

The algebraic equation is _____ .

How many flying discs are in the barrel? _____

Talk About It
Complete the sentences.

3. In Problem 1, $6 \times \triangle$ is an ...

4. In Problem 2, d is a ...

5. The value of d is _____.

6. In both problems I solved algebraic ...

Your Turn
Talk with a partner. Share what you have learned about variables.

Variables **47**

Think, Talk, and Write

Your Turn

Each bag holds the same number of jump ropes. How many jump ropes are in each bag?

4 of the same bags

28 jump ropes in all

Use the variable *j* to represent the number of jump ropes in each bag.

An algebraic expression for all of the jump ropes is _____ .

An algebraic equation is _____ .

The value of *j* is _____ .

There are _____ jump ropes in each bag.

Talk and Write About It

Complete the sentences about the problems you solved.

Vocabulary		
variable	equal	algebraic equation
expression	equation	algebraic expression
missing number	solve	inverse operations

1. In the problem, *j* is a _____ .

2. The equation has an _____ sign.

3. 5 × *r* is an _____ .

4. When you find the value of the variable, you _____ the equation.

Produce Language

Write the terms you learned about in this lesson in the third column of the chart on page 45. Write what you have learned about these terms. Use sentence starters from throughout the lesson for support.

The Coordinate Plane

Essential Question What terms do you need to use and understand when you discuss the coordinate plane?

You Will

- Find points on the coordinate plane.
- Name points on the coordinate plane.
- Use math vocabulary to discuss the coordinate plane.

Talk About It

Make an index card for each vocabulary term below. Place each card in one of three piles.

Pile 1 I know what this term means.
Pile 2 I have heard of this term, but I am not sure how it is used in math.
Pile 3 I have not heard of this term.

ordered pair

integers	negative integer	positive integer
coordinate plane	point	ordered pair
y-axis	*y*-coordinate	*x*-axis
x-coordinate	origin	quadrant
coordinates		

What do you know about each term? Explain, using the sentence starters for support.

I know … means …
I think … means …
I do not know what … means.

Your Turn

Look at the objectives under You Will at the top of the page. Working with a partner, predict what you are going to learn. Use the sentence starter for support.

I am going to learn about …

Vocabulary in Context **Picture It!**

coordinate plane

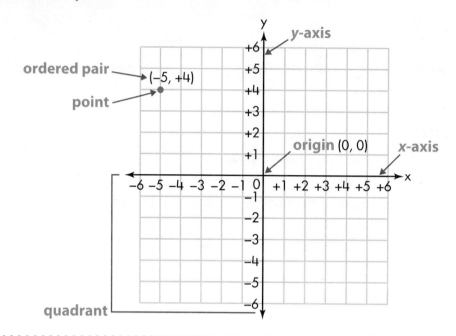

Talk About It 💬

Talk with a partner. Complete the sentences.

1. The numbers −1, −3, and −6 are all …

2. A coordinate plane has four …

3. The *x*-axis and *y*-axis cross at the …

4. In the ordered pair (−6, +3), the integer +3 is the …

5. In the ordered pair (−4, +1), the integer −4 is the …

Your Turn 💬

Draw a point on the coordinate plane. Tell a partner as much as you can about the point. Use the sentence starters for help.

The ordered pair is …

The *y*-coordinate is …

Look at the city map. Fill in the missing coordinates.

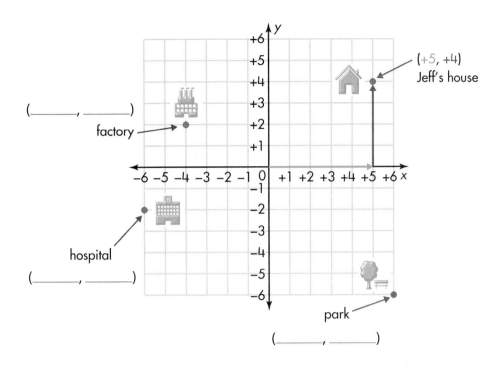

(_____, _____)

factory

(_____, _____)

hospital

(+5, +4)
Jeff's house

(_____, _____)

park

Talk About It

Complete the sentences about the city map.

1 Each location on the map is described by an ...

2 Both coordinates for Jeff's House are ...

3 The park is 6 units below the ...

4 The point at (0, 0) is called the ...

5 The x-coordinate for the hospital is a ...

6 The map is drawn on the ...

Your Turn

Choose an x-coordinate and a y-coordinate from the lists below. Tell a partner how to use the two coordinates to draw a point on the coordinate plane.

x-coordinate						y-coordinate				
−5	−3	−1	+2	+3		−6	−4	−2	+4	+5

Think, Talk, and Write

Your Turn

Four families are planning a camping trip. A map of the campground is drawn on the coordinate plane. Help the families plan where to set up their four tents. Put each one in a different quadrant. Draw a point and write the ordered pair.

(_____ , _____)

(_____ , _____)

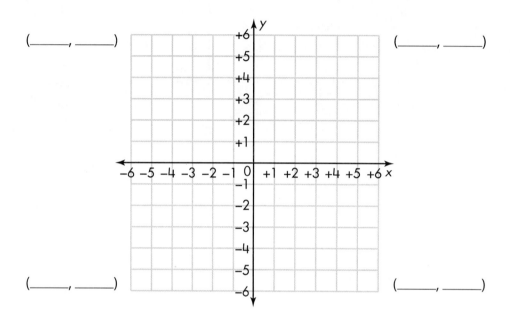

(_____ , _____)

(_____ , _____)

Talk and Write About It

Complete the sentences.

Vocabulary

y-coordinate	x-axis	coordinate plane
y-axis	origin	ordered pair
x-coordinate	point	

1. An ordered pair gives the location of a point on the _____ .

2. The second number in an ordered pair is the _____ .

3. The origin is where the x-axis crosses the _____ .

Produce Language

Write about how positive and negative integers can help you find places on the coordinate plane. Use as many vocabulary terms as you can. Share with a partner.

Graphs of Equations

Essential Question What vocabulary will help you understand and talk about graphs of equations?

You Will

- Given an equation, complete a table of values and plot the ordered pairs.
- Describe how graphs represent the relationship between two variables.
- Use math vocabulary to discuss variables.

Talk About It

Copy each term from Vocabulary in Context on a card. As your teacher reads each term, create three piles of cards.

1. Place terms that you know in **Pile 1**.

2. Place terms you have heard but are not sure what they mean in **Pile 2**.

3. Place terms you do not know in **Pile 3**.

What do you know about each term? Explain, using the sentence starters for support.

I know … means …
I think … means …
I do not know what … means.

x-axis

ordered pair

coordinate grid

Your Turn

Look at the objectives under You Will at the top of the page. Working with a partner, predict what you are going to learn. Use the sentence starter for support.

I am going to learn about …

Vocabulary in Context **Picture It!**

variables

$6 + c$ $\Box \div 3$

ordered pair

$(3, 6)$

x-coordinate   *y*-coordinate

plot Mark a point on a coordinate grid.

table of values

Hours walked x	Miles walked y
1	2
2	4
3	6

x-values   *y*-values

coordinate grid

y-axis

point

x-axis

origin

graph of
linear equation
$y = 2x$

Talk About It

Talk with a partner. Complete the sentences.

1. In the table, 3 is an …

2. The point (0, 0) is the …

3. (3, 6) is an …

4. In the ordered pair (5, 10), 10 is the …

Your Turn

Choose a term on this page. Write what it means to you. Share with a partner what you know about it. Use the sentence starter for help.

I think … means …

Do You Understand?

Lynn is 3 years older than Pete. This story is shown in the table. This story is also shown in the graph and by the linear equation $y = x + 3$.

Pete's age x	Lynn's age y
1	4
3	6
5	8
7	10

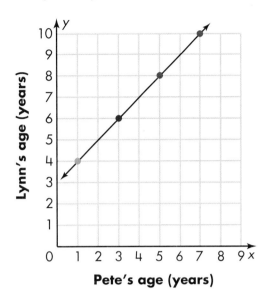

Pete's age (years)

1. When Pete is 1, Lynn is 4. What ordered pair shows their ages?

   (_____, _____)

2. When Pete is 5, Lynn is 8. What is the ordered pair? (_____, _____)

3. When Pete is 6, how old is Lynn? _____ What is the ordered pair?

   (_____, _____) Plot the point on the coordinate grid that shows that ordered pair.

4. Give the ordered pair for another point on the line. (_____, _____)

   That ordered pair shows that Pete's age is _____ and Lynn's age is

   _____ .

Talk About It
Complete the sentences.

5. In the table, the values 1, 3, 5, and 7 are the …

6. The line is the graph of a …

Your Turn
Look at Problem 3. Write how you found the answers. Use the table and coordinate grid to help you.

Graphs of Equations   **55**

Think, Talk, and Write

Your Turn

Seth is 2 years older than Maria.
The linear equation that shows this is $y = x + 2$.

Write the missing values in the table below. Then graph the ordered pairs and draw a line through the points.

Maria x	Seth y
2	4
3	
4	
6	
7	

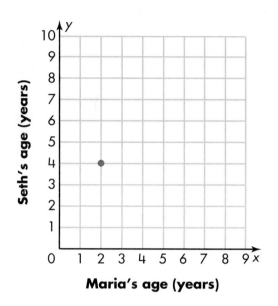

Maria's age (years)

Talk and Write About It

Complete the sentences about the table and the grid.

Vocabulary

variables	y-values	graph	table of values
coordinate grid	x-values	y-coordinate	ordered pair
linear equation	x-coordinate	origin	point

1 The graph is drawn on a _____ .

2 x and y are _____ .

3 The values in the column for Seth's age are _____ .

Produce Language

Write about what you have learned about graphing equations. You may include examples. Use as many vocabulary terms and symbols as you can.

Points, Lines, and Angles

Essential Question What vocabulary terms will help you describe points, lines, and angles?

You Will
- Recognize the properties of points, lines, and angles.
- Understand the relationship among points, lines, and angles.
- Use math vocabulary to describe points, lines, and angles.

Talk About It

Look at the list of terms below. In the first two columns of the chart, write terms you **know** or **want** to know more about.

line   intersecting lines   angle
line segment   perpendicular lines   vertex
horizontal line   parallel lines   ray
vertical line   point of intersection

Know	Want	Learned

What do you know about each term? Explain, using the sentence starters for support.

I know … means …
I want to know more about …

Your Turn

Look at the objectives under You Will at the top of the page. Working with a partner, predict what you are going to learn. Use the sentence starter for support.

I am going to learn about …

Vocabulary in Context **Picture It!**

line

ray

line segment

horizontal line

vertical line

angle

vertex

intersecting lines

point of intersection

perpendicular lines

parallel lines

Talk About It

Talk with a partner. Complete the sentences.

1. Part of a line that stops at each end is a …
2. Part of a line that continues in only one direction is a …
3. The point where two or more lines meet is a …
4. Lines that form square corners are …

Your Turn

Choose three terms on this page. Draw an example of each. Share your drawings with a partner. Ask your partner to describe them.

Do You Understand?

Look at the map of Kim's neighborhood. Use vocabulary terms to describe the map.

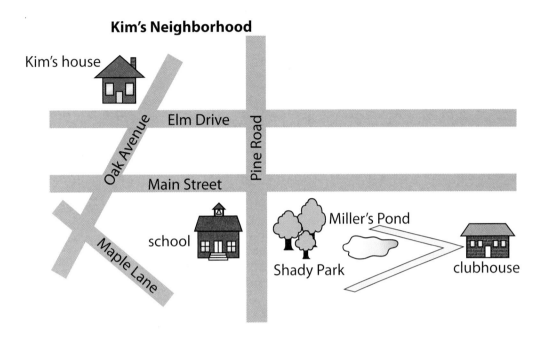

Kim's Neighborhood

Kim's house

Oak Avenue

Elm Drive

Pine Road

Main Street

Maple Lane

school

Shady Park

Miller's Pond

clubhouse

1. The streets that cross at Kim's house look like _____.

2. The path at Miller's Pond looks like an _____.

3. The clubhouse at Miller's Pond is near the angle's _____.

Talk About It
Complete the sentences to help describe Kim's neighborhood.

4. Elm Drive and Main Street look like …

5. The streets that cross at the school look like …

6. Streets that cross each other and form square corners look like …

7. Oak Avenue and Maple Lane look like …

Your Turn
Draw a street that crosses Maple Lane. Describe the new street. Tell a partner using vocabulary terms.

Your Turn

Draw a neighborhood street map. Write a name on each street. Be sure
your picture includes examples of at least five of the terms shown in the
vocabulary box below.

Talk and Write About It

Complete the sentences.

Vocabulary			
lines	intersecting lines	angle	line segment
vertex	horizontal line	ray	parallel lines
vertical line	perpendicular lines		

1 Two streets that cross look like _____ .

2 Two streets that cross and form square corners look like

_____ .

3 A street on a map that goes from left to right looks like a

_____ .

Produce Language

Write the terms you learned about in this lesson in the third column of the
chart on page 57. Then write what you have learned about points, lines,
and angles.

Measuring Angles

Essential Question How can you use vocabulary terms to discuss measuring angles?

You Will
- Identify parts of an angle.
- Measure and classify angles.
- Use math vocabulary to discuss angles.

Talk About It

Rate these mathematical terms according to the following scale.

1. I have never heard this term.

2. I have heard this term, but I do not know how to use it in math.

3. I understand the meaning of this term and know how to use it in math.

_____ angle   _____ degrees

_____ straight angle   _____ congruent

_____ vertex   _____ right angle

_____ side   _____ acute angle

_____ protractor   _____ obtuse angle

_____ measure

Explain what you know about each term, using the sentence starters.

I do not know what … means.
I think … means …
I know … means …

Your Turn

Look at the objectives under You Will at the top of the page. Working with a partner, predict what you are going to learn. Use the sentence starter for support.

I am going to learn about …

angle
∠BAC (∠CAB or ∠A)

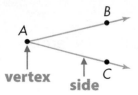

vertex   side

protractor

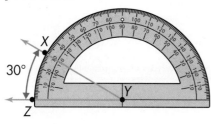

The **measure** of ∠XYZ is
30 **degrees** (30˚).

congruent

right angle

90º

acute angle

less than 90º

obtuse angle

between 90º and 180º

straight angle

180°

Talk About It

Talk with a partner. Complete the sentences.

1. The symbol ˚ means …
2. An angle with a measure of 90 degrees is a …
3. Two angles that are the same size are …
4. The point where two sides of an angle meet is a …
5. Angles are measured in …
6. Another name for ∠STU at the right is …

Your Turn

Draw four different types of angles. Share your drawings with a partner.
Ask your partner to describe them.

Do You Understand?

1. Look at the angles marked in the bicycle frame.
Write whether the angles are acute or obtuse.
The first angle is done for you.

∠*ABC* is obtuse.

_____

_____

_____

_____

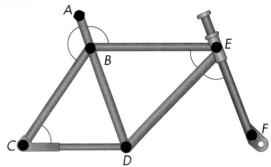

2. Use your protractor to measure each angle below.
Write the measure. Then write if the angle is right, acute,
straight, or obtuse.

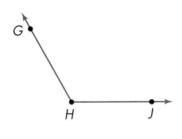

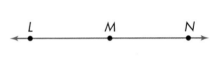

_____

_____

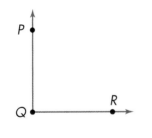

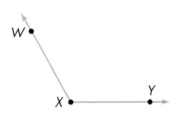

_____

_____

Talk About It

Complete the sentences to describe the angles.

3. In the bike frame, ∠*BDE* is an …

4. ∠*GHJ* and ∠*WXY* are …

5. In ∠*PQR*, point *Q* is the …

6. An angle with a measure of 180 degrees is a …

Your Turn

Draw an angle. Measure it with a protractor. Describe your angle to a partner.
Use vocabulary terms to help you.

Your Turn

Look at the frame of the house. Measure at least ten angles. Then draw a heart ♥ inside a right angle, a star ★ inside an acute angle, and a circle ● inside an obtuse angle.

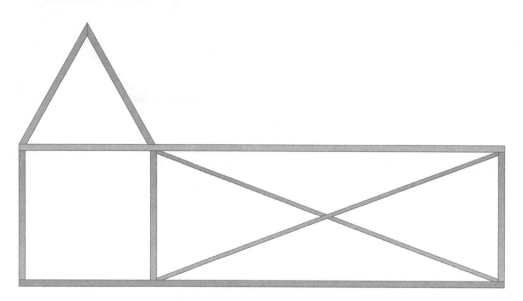

Talk and Write About It

Complete the sentences about measuring angles.

> **Vocabulary**
>
> vertex   degrees   measure   straight angle
> congruent   protractor   obtuse angle   acute angle
> right angle   side

1. When I measure angles, I use a _____ .

2. If two angles both measure 60°, the angles are _____ .

3. An angle with a measure between 90° and 180° is an _____ .

4. Angles are classified as acute, right, obtuse, or _____ .

Produce Language

Write how measuring angles helps you find out about different kinds of angles. Use as many vocabulary terms as you can.

Properties of Shapes

Essential Question What vocabulary terms should you use to talk about the properties of shapes?

You Will
- Identify the properties of shapes.
- Classify shapes.
- Use math vocabulary to discuss the properties of shapes.

Talk About It

Copy each term from Vocabulary in Context on a card. As your teacher reads each term, create three piles of cards.

1. Place terms that you know in **Pile 1.**
2. Place terms you have heard but are not sure what they mean in **Pile 2.**
3. Place terms you do not know in **Pile 3.**

What do you know about each term? Explain, using the sentence starters for support.

I know … means …
I think … means …
I do not know what … means.

square

pentagon

quadrilateral

Your Turn
Look at the objectives listed under You Will at the top of the page. Working with a partner, predict what you will learn. Use the sentence starter below.

I am going to learn about …

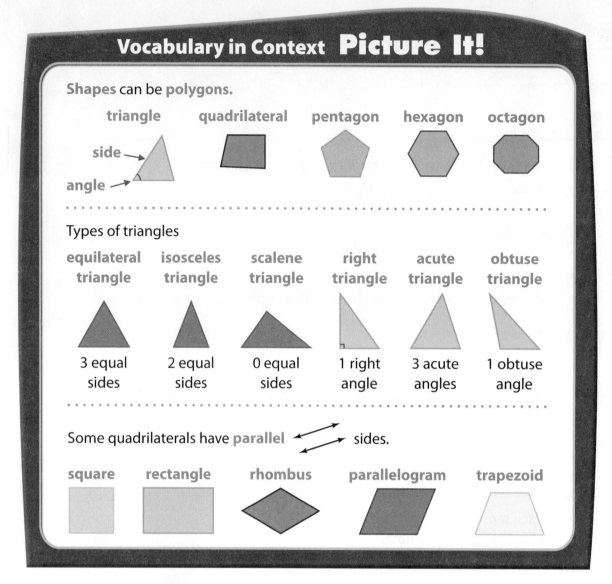

Shapes can be **polygons.**

triangle quadrilateral pentagon hexagon octagon

side
angle

Types of triangles

equilateral triangle	isosceles triangle	scalene triangle	right triangle	acute triangle	obtuse triangle
3 equal sides	2 equal sides	0 equal sides	1 right angle	3 acute angles	1 obtuse angle

Some quadrilaterals have **parallel** sides.

square rectangle rhombus parallelogram trapezoid

Talk About It

Talk with a partner. Complete the sentences.

1. Shapes that have four sides are called ...

2. A triangle that has one obtuse angle is an ...

3. Pentagons and octagons are ...

4. A rectangle has two pairs of ... sides.

Your Turn

Draw a quadrilateral and a triangle. Describe them to a partner. Include as many vocabulary terms as you can.

Look at the angles, triangles, and quadrilaterals in the spider web below.

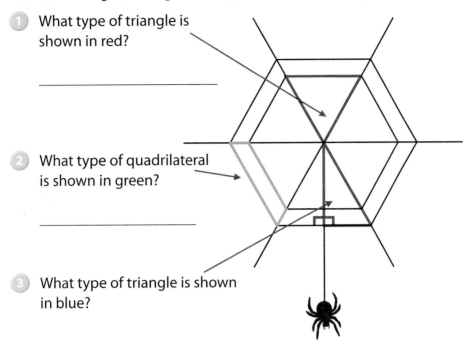

1   What type of triangle is shown in red?

_____

2   What type of quadrilateral is shown in green?

_____

3   What type of triangle is shown in blue?

_____

Take a look at the shapes below. Write the missing angle measures. Use these two properties:

• The sum of the measures of the angles in a triangle is 180°.
• The sum of the measures of the angles in a quadrilateral is 360°.

4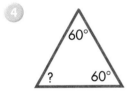

5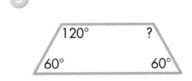

6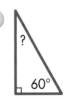

Talk About It
Complete the sentences to describe the shapes.

7   An equilateral triangle is also an …

8   A trapezoid has one pair of … sides.

9   A triangle with a right angle is a …

Your Turn
Draw your own spider web design. Use vocabulary terms to tell your partner about some of the shapes in your design.

Your Turn

Look at the quilt square shown below.

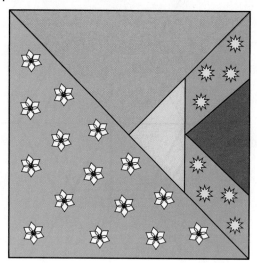

1 How many parallelograms are there? _____

2 What do the yellow triangle and bright blue triangle have in common?

_____

3 Are there any equilateral triangles in the quilt square? _____

4 Are there any obtuse triangles in the quilt square? _____

Talk and Write About It

Complete the sentences about shapes.

hexagon	quadrilaterals	isosceles triangle
trapezoid	rectangle	parallelogram
square	rhombus	equilateral triangle
right angle	right triangle	acute angle

5 A quadrilateral with four equal sides is a _____ .

6 A polygon with six sides is a _____ .

7 A triangle with two equal sides is an _____ .

Produce Language

Use vocabulary terms to write about shapes that have one or more right angles. Then write about shapes that have parallel sides.

Converting Units of Measure

Essential Question How can you use vocabulary terms to talk about converting units of measure?

You Will

- Use customary and metric units of measure to solve problems.
- Convert measurements from one unit of measure to another.
- Use math vocabulary to discuss converting units of measure.

Talk About It

Make an index card for each vocabulary term below. Place each card in one of three piles.

Pile 1: I know what this term means.
Pile 2: I have heard of this term, but I am not sure how it is used in math.
Pile 3: I have not heard of this term.

unit of measure

customary units	capacity	gallon (gal)	quart (qt)
pint (pt)	kilometer (km)	ton (T)	pound (lb)
ounce (oz)	yard (yd)	foot (ft)	inch (in.)
metric units	liter (L)	milliliter (mL)	mass
kilogram (kg)	millimeter (mm)	milligram (mg)	meter (m)
centimeter (cm)	weight	fluid ounce (fl oz)	gram (g)
unit of measure	length	mile (mi)	cup (c)
convert			

What do you know about each term? Explain, using the sentence starters for support.

I know … means …
I think … means …
I do not know what … means.

Your Turn

Look at the objectives under You Will at the top of the page. Working with a partner, predict what you are going to learn. Use the sentence starter for support.

I am going to learn about …

Vocabulary in Context **Picture It!**

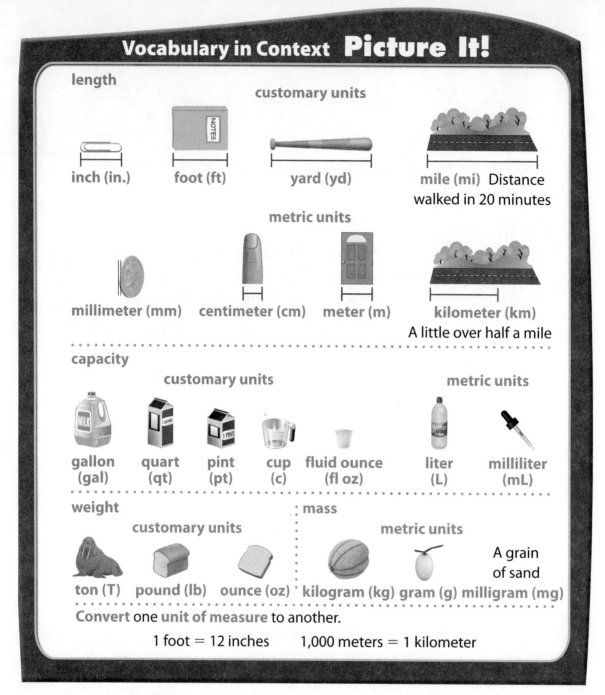

length

customary units

inch (in.) foot (ft) yard (yd) mile (mi) Distance walked in 20 minutes

metric units

millimeter (mm) centimeter (cm) meter (m) kilometer (km)

A little over half a mile

capacity

customary units

gallon (gal) quart (qt) pint (pt) cup (c) fluid ounce (fl oz)

metric units

liter (L) milliliter (mL)

weight

customary units

mass

metric units

A grain of sand

ton (T) pound (lb) ounce (oz) kilogram (kg) gram (g) milligram (mg)

Convert one **unit of measure** to another.

1 foot = 12 inches   1,000 meters = 1 kilometer

Talk About It

Talk with a partner. Complete the sentences.

1. Liters and milliliters are … of capacity.

2. T is the abbreviation for …

3. Inches and meters are units of …

Your Turn

Choose a unit of weight. Tell a partner two objects you could measure with that unit.

Match each picture with the correct unit of measure from the box. Write the unit underneath the picture.

cups   tons   milliliters   feet   millimeters   ounces

 1 _____   2 _____   3 _____   4 _____

Use the Measurement Table (page 95) to help you convert each measurement.

5   7 yd = _____ ft

6   20 kg = _____ g

7   5 c = _____ fl oz

8   300 m = _____ cm

9   16 qt = _____ gal

10   1.8 L = _____ mL

Talk About It
Complete the sentences below.

11   Use gallons and liters to measure …

12   One yard equals 36 …

13   Thirty-two ounces converts to 2 …

Your Turn
Write the units of measure given in the box at the top of the page. Write down an object you could measure using each unit. Share your ideas with a partner.

Your Turn

Use the Measurement Tables (page 95) to help you complete the following.

1 This building is 240 yards tall. How many feet is that?

_____ ft

2 Macy bought 2 gallons of milk. How many pints of milk is this?

_____ pt

3 How many inches is 12 feet of rope? _____ in.

4 What is the diameter in centimeters of one U.S. quarter? _____ cm

5 What is the diameter in millimeters of one U.S. quarter? _____ mm

6 One U.S. quarter has a mass of 5.67 grams. What is the mass of a U.S. quarter in milligrams? _____ mg

Talk and Write About It

Complete the sentences about the measurements.

Vocabulary			
customary units	capacity	milliliter	mass
metric units	weight	pounds	feet
yards	length	kilograms	gallons

7 Pounds and tons are units of _____ .

8 Grams and kilograms are units of _____ .

9 Yards and miles are _____ of length.

10 Thirty-six inches converts to 3 _____ .

Produce Language

Suppose you have a pet. Write about some things you could measure that are related to your pet and caring for your pet. Use your vocabulary cards for support.

Perimeter and Area

Essential Question What words should you use to talk about area and perimeter?

You Will

- Find the perimeter and area of triangles and rectangles.
- Use formulas to find the perimeter and area of triangles and rectangles.
- Use math vocabulary to discuss perimeter and area.

Talk About It

Look at the list of terms below. In the first two columns of the chart, write terms you **know** or **want** to know more about.

square inch   unit   square foot   formulas
square centimeter   square meter   area   square unit
dimensions   base   height   perimeter
length   width   distance

Know	Want	Learned

What do you know about each term you wrote in the chart? Explain, using the sentence starters for support.

I know … means …
I want to know more about …

Your Turn

Look at the objectives under You Will at the top of the page. Working with a partner, predict what you are going to learn. Use the sentence starter for support.

I am going to learn about …

Vocabulary in Context Picture It!

perimeter The **distance** around a shape

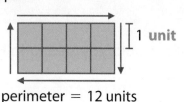

perimeter = 12 units

area The number of square units needed to cover a shape

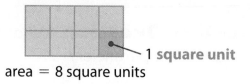

1 **square unit**

area = 8 square units

square units

      square centimeter (cm²)   **square inch (in²)**

      square foot (ft²)   **square meter (m²)**

dimensions

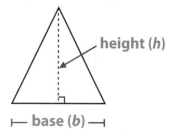

height (h)

base (b)

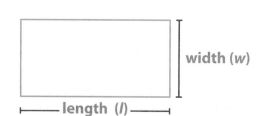

width (w)

length (l)

Area = $\frac{1}{2}$ × base × height

$A = \frac{1}{2} \times b \times h$

formulas

Area = length × width

$A = l \times w$

Perimeter = (2 × length) + (2 × width)

$P = (2 \times l) + (2 \times w)$

Talk About It

Talk with a partner. Complete the sentences.

1. The distance around a shape is the …

2. $A = l \times w$ is a …

3. The number of square units needed to cover a shape is the …

Your Turn

Draw a shape that has all straight sides. Explain to a partner how to find the perimeter. Use as many vocabulary terms as you can.

Sari has a small blue cloth in the shape of a rectangle. It is pictured on page 97. Tear out page 97 and cut out the rectangle.

Help Sari find the area and perimeter of the rectangle.

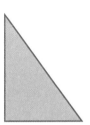

On the picture at the right, write the dimensions of the rectangle you cut out.

The length is 9 centimeters. The width is _____ .

Area = length × _____

The area of the rectangle is _____ .

Perimeter = (2 × _____) + (2 × width)

The perimeter is _____ .

Cut the rectangle in half from corner to corner.

Sari wants to know the area of each triangle. So she divides the area of the rectangle by 2.

108 square centimeters ÷ 2 = _____ square centimeters.

Sari's sister finds the area of the triangle by using the formula.

On the picture at the right, write the dimensions of one of the triangles.

The base is 9 centimeters. The height is _____ .

Area = $\frac{1}{2}$ × base × _____

The area of each triangle is _____ .

Talk About It

Complete the sentences below.

1. An equation you use to find the area of a shape is called a …

2. The dimensions of a rectangle are the length and the …

3. $P = (2 \times l) + (2 \times w)$ is the formula for the … of a rectangle.

Your Turn

Look at one of the triangles you cut. The length of the longest side is 15 centimeters. Explain to your partner how you can find the perimeter of the triangle.

Your Turn

Find the perimeter of each shape.

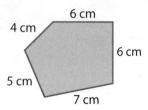

6 cm
4 cm
6 cm
5 cm
7 cm

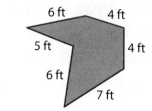

6 ft   4 ft
5 ft   4 ft
6 ft
7 ft

_____   _____

Find the area and perimeter of each shape.

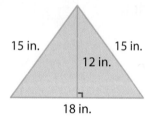

15 in.   15 in.
12 in.
18 in.

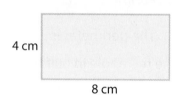

4 cm
8 cm

_____   _____

_____   _____

Talk and Write About It

Complete the sentences about area and perimeter.

Vocabulary			
square inches	square feet	area	base
square meters	dimensions	perimeter	height

5. $A = \frac{1}{2} \times b \times h$ is the formula for the _____ of a triangle.

6. The distance around a shape is the _____ .

7. If length and width of a rectangle are measured in meters, then

   the area is measured in _____ .

Produce Language

Write the terms you learned about in this lesson in the third column of the chart on page 73. Then write and draw pictures to explain what you have learned about area and perimeter.

Surface Area and Volume

Essential Question How do you use vocabulary terms to discuss surface area and volume?

You Will
- Find surface area and volume of rectangular prisms.
- Use math vocabulary to discuss surface area and volume.

Talk About It

Rate these mathematical terms according to the following scale.

1 I do not know this term.

2 I have heard this term, but I do not know how to use it in math.

3 I understand this term and I know how to use it in math.

_____ net   _____ volume

_____ cube   _____ cubic unit

_____ rectangular prism   _____ solid figure

_____ face   _____ area

_____ edge   _____ length

_____ square unit   _____ width

_____ vertex   _____ height

_____ surface area

Explain what you know about each term, using the sentence starters.

I do not know what … means.
I think … means …
I know … means … in math.

Your Turn
Look at the objectives under You Will at the top of the page. Working with a partner, predict what you are going to learn. Use the sentence starter for support.

I am going to learn about …

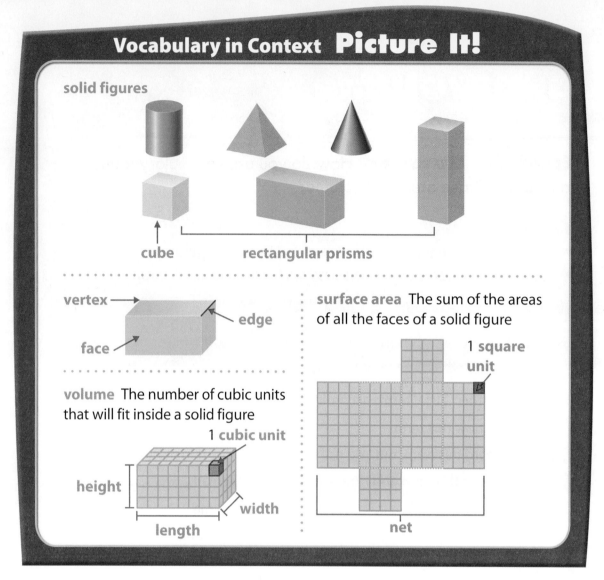

solid figures

cube

rectangular prisms

vertex → edge

face

surface area The sum of the areas of all the faces of a solid figure

1 square unit

volume The number of cubic units that will fit inside a solid figure

1 cubic unit

height

width

length

net

Talk About It

Talk with a partner. Complete the sentences.

1. Rectangular prisms are …
2. A rectangular prism has six …
3. The area of a surface is measured in …
4. The volume of a solid figure is measured in …
5. When folded, a … makes a solid figure.

Your Turn

Choose a solid figure in your classroom to describe. Use vocabulary terms. Share your description with your partner.

Use the Solid Shape Patterns (page 99) to help you build the cubic unit and a rectangular prism.

Step 1 Cut out the net of the cubic unit.

Step 2 Fold on the dotted lines.

Step 3 Tape the net to form the cubic unit. It has a volume of one cubic unit.

Step 4 Cut out the net of the rectangular prism.

Step 5 Fold on the dotted lines. You want the grid lines on the outside of the rectangular prism.

Step 6 Tape the net to form the rectangular prism.

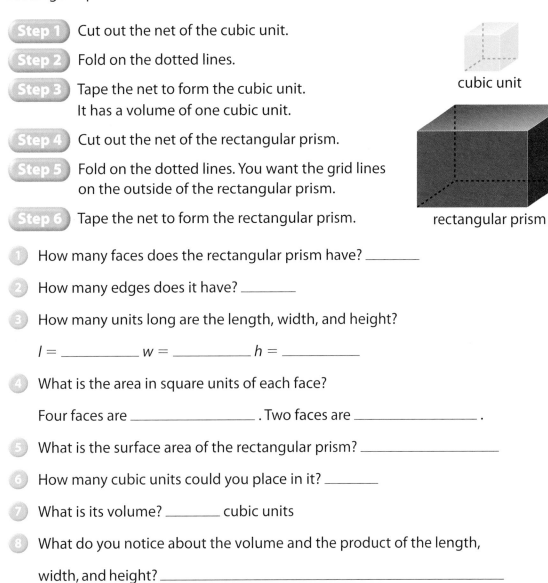

cubic unit

rectangular prism

1. How many faces does the rectangular prism have? _____

2. How many edges does it have? _____

3. How many units long are the length, width, and height?

   $l =$ _____ $w =$ _____ $h =$ _____

4. What is the area in square units of each face?

   Four faces are _____ . Two faces are _____ .

5. What is the surface area of the rectangular prism? _____

6. How many cubic units could you place in it? _____

7. What is its volume? _____ cubic units

8. What do you notice about the volume and the product of the length,

   width, and height? _____

Talk About It
Complete the sentences below.

9. The total number of cubic units in a solid figure is the …

10. A rectangular prism and a cube each have 6 …

11. The number of square units on the surface of a solid figure is the …

Your Turn
Write about how the cube and the rectangular prism are the same and how they are different. Use as many vocabulary terms as you can. Share your answers with a partner.

Your Turn

The net shown below can be used to make the rectangular prism.

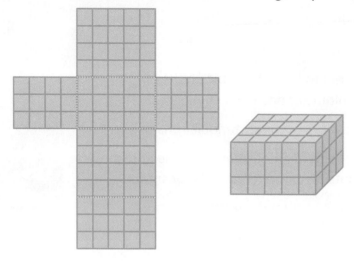

1. How long is the rectangular prism? _____

2. How wide is it? _____

3. How high is it? _____

4. What is its volume? _____

5. What is its surface area? _____

Talk and Write About It

Complete the sentences about solid figures.

Vocabulary			
net	vertex	edge	cube
surface area	rectangular prism	volume	face
cubic unit	square unit		

6. A figure that looks like a box is a _____ .

7. Each corner of a rectangular prism is called a _____ .

8. Each flat surface of a rectangular prism is called a _____ .

Produce Language

Write something you learned about surface area. Write something you learned about volume. Use the Vocabulary in Context Picture It! for support. Share with a partner.

Mean, Median, and Mode

Essential Question
What vocabulary terms will help you understand mean, median, and mode?

You Will
- Find the median, mean, and mode of a set of data.
- Find the minimum, maximum, and range of a set of data.
- Use vocabulary terms to discuss mean, median, and mode.

Talk About It

Copy each term from Vocabulary in Context on a card. As your teacher reads each term, create three piles of cards.

1. Place terms that you know in **Pile 1.**

2. Place terms you have heard but are not sure what they mean in **Pile 2.**

3. Place terms you do not know in **Pile 3.**

What do you know about each term? Explain, using the sentence starters for support.

I know … means …
I think … means …
I do not know what … means.

average

median

mode

Your Turn
Look at the objectives under You Will at the top of the page. Working with a partner, predict what you are going to learn. Use the sentence starter for support.

I am going to learn about …

data Collected information

Number of Absences				
Monday	Tuesday	Wednesday	Thursday	Friday
1	4	7	9	9

The **value** for Tuesday is 4.

data set (or **set of data**)

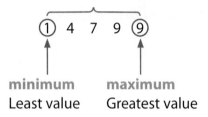

minimum
Least value

maximum
Greatest value

range The difference between the maximum and minimum

$9 - 1 = \boxed{8}$

mean (average) The sum of the values divided by the number of values

$1 + 4 + 7 + 9 + 9 = 30$

$30 \div 5 = \boxed{6}$

median The middle vlaue

1　4　⑦　9　9

mode The value that occurs most often

1　4　7　⑨　⑨

Talk About It

Complete the sentences with a partner.

1. The value that occurs most often is the …

2. When the values in a set of data are arranged in order, the value that is in the middle is the …

3. The least value in a set of data is the …

4. The greatest value in a set of data is the …

5. The average of a set of data is also called the …

Your Turn

Choose a term on this page. Think about what it means to you. Share with a partner. Use the sentence starter for support.

I think … means …

The table below shows the number of minutes Arturo swam each day for 5 days.

Minutes Arturo Swam	
Day	**Number of Minutes**
Monday	20
Tuesday	25
Wednesday	14
Thursday	25
Friday	11

1. Write the data in order from least to greatest.

   _____, _____, _____, _____, _____

2. What is the minimum number of minutes Arturo swam? _____

3. What is the maximum number of minutes Arturo swam? _____

4. What is the difference between the maximum and the minimum?

   That number is the range. _____

5. What value occurs most often? That number is the mode. _____

6. What value is in the middle? That number is the median. _____

7. Add all the values. Then divide the sum by the number of values.

   The result is the mean. _____

Talk About It
Complete the sentences.

8. The mean of a set of data is also called the …

9. If a data set has all different values, there is no …

10. To find the range, subtract the maximum minus the …

Your Turn
Write what you know about finding the mean of a set of data. Then tell a partner what you know about the mean.

Mean, Median, and Mode   **83**

Your Turn

The table below shows the number of books some students read.

Books Read	
Name	**Number of Books**
Olivia	8
Jamie	5
Adam	1
Enrique	5
Leah	10
Josh	5
Isabella	8

1. What is the minimum number of books read? _____

2. What is the maximum number of books read? _____

3. What is the range of the data? _____

4. What is the mean number of books read? _____

5. What is the median number of books read? _____

6. What is the mode? _____

Talk and Write About It

Complete the sentences.

Vocabulary

mean	median	mode	minimum
maximum	range	average	data
data set	value		

7. The value that occurs most often is the _____ .

8. The mean is also called the _____ .

9. The difference between the minimum and maximum is the _____ .

10. The value that is in the middle of the data is the _____ .

Produce Language

Write directions for how to solve Problem 5.

Graphs

Essential Question How can you talk about different types of graphs?

You Will
- Interpret and label circle graphs.
- Construct and interpret line plots, line graphs, and bar graphs.
- Use math vocabulary to discuss different types of graphs.

Talk About It

Look at the list of terms below. In the first two columns of the chart, write terms you **know** or **want** to know more about.

data	frequency	frequency table	line plot
picture graph	key	bar graph	line graph
trend	circle graph		

Know	Want	Learned

What do you know about each term? Explain, using the sentence starters for support.

I know … means …
I want to know more about …

Your Turn
Look at the objectives under You Will at the top of the page. Working with a partner, predict what you are going to learn. Use the sentence starter for support.

I am going to learn about …

Vocabulary in Context **Picture It!**

frequency table

Pets per Student

Pets per Student	
0 pets	4
1 pets	2
2 pets	3
3 pets	2

data

line plot

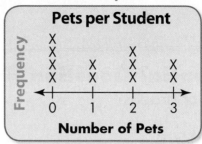

picture graph

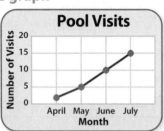

key

bar graph

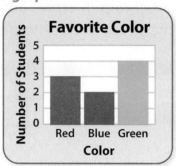

line graph

Pool Visits

trend: The number of visits increased each month.

circle graph

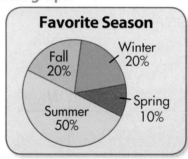

Talk About It

Talk with a partner. Complete the sentences.

1. In a line plot, the Xs above a number show the …

2. A graph that uses pictures to show data is a …

3. A graph of points connected by line segments is a …

Your Turn

Choose three of the graphs above. Write a sentence about how each graph shows data. Talk about your ideas in a small group.

1 How many books did Grade 4 donate?

Book Donations

Grade	Number of Books
Grade 3	📘📘📘
Grade 4	📘📘
Grade 5	📘📘📘📘📘

Key: 📘 = 50 books

2 How many students have an arm length of 25 inches?

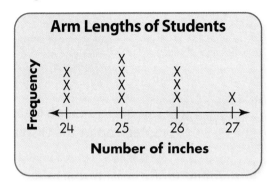

3 Which team won the most medals?

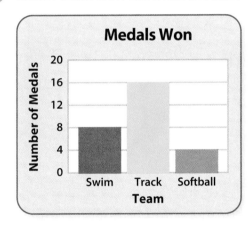

4 What trend does this graph show?

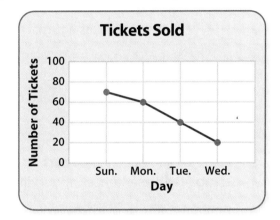

Talk About It
Complete the sentences about graphs.

5 The graph in Problem 1 is a …

6 The graph in Problem 2 is a …

7 The graph in Problem 3 is a …

8 The graph in Problem 4 is a …

Your Turn
Choose two of the graphs above. Tell your partner how they are different.

Think, Talk, and Write

Your Turn

Work with a partner to complete the Graph Matching card game.

Display **Term**

Step 1 Cut out the Graph Matching Activity cards from pages 101–104. Spread apart the Display cards and place them facedown in front of Player 1.

Step 2 Spread apart the Term cards and place them facedown in front of Player 2.

Step 3 Player 1 chooses a Display card and a Term card and turns them faceup. Player 1 keeps the pair if they match. Player 1 turns them facedown again if they do not match.

Step 4 Player 2 takes a turn.

Step 5 Repeat Steps 3 and 4 until all cards have been paired.

Work with your partner and take turns asking each other questions about the data on each Display card.

Talk and Write About It

Complete the sentences about different types of graphs.

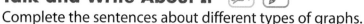

Vocabulary			
data	frequency	key	line plot
picture graph	bar graph	line graph	circle graph

1. A graph is a display of _____ .

2. Connected line segments can show the trend of the data in a

    _____ .

3. A graph with Xs drawn above a number line is a _____ .

4. In a picture graph, the value of each picture is told in the _____ .

Produce Language

Write the terms you learned about in this lesson in the third column of the chart on page 85. Then write a sentence about each table or graph in this lesson.

My Addition & Subtraction Words

Addition

add _____

plus (+) _____

sum _____

total _____

addend _____

_____

_____

_____

_____

Subtraction

subtract _____

minus (−) _____

difference _____

fewer than _____

left _____

_____

_____

_____

_____

My Multiplication & Division Words

Multiplication

multiply _____

times (×) _____

product _____

factors _____

array _____

_____

_____

_____

_____

Division

divide _____

divided by (÷) _____

quotient _____

divisor _____

dividend _____

_____

_____

_____

_____

School Shopping
Four Corners Activity

Corner 1

Paste your card(s) here:

What is the total cost of 4?

(HINT: **Multiply** the cost by 4.)

Corner 2

Paste your card(s) here:

What is the **sum**?

School Shopping
Four Corners Activity

Paste your card(s) here:

How many can you buy for $3.00?

(HINT: **Divide** $3.00 by the cost.)

Paste your card(s) here:

What is the **difference** in costs?

School Shopping
Four Corners Activity Cards

Cut out each school supply card. Then follow the directions on pages 91–92.

$0.50	$0.65	$0.15
$0.15	$1.20	$0.75
$0.85	$0.45	$0.30

Measurement Tables

Units of Length

Customary

1 foot = 12 inches (in.)

1 yard (yd) = 3 feet (ft)

1 yard = 36 in.

1 mile (mi) = 1,760 yards

1 mile = 5,280 ft

Metric

1 centimeter = 10 millimeters (mm)

1 meter = 100 centimeters (cm)

1 meter = 1,000 mm

1 kilometer (km) = 1,000 meters (m)

Units of Capacity

Customary

1 cup = 8 fluid ounces (fl oz)

1 pint = 2 cups (c)

1 quart = 2 pints (pt)

1 gallon (gal) = 4 quarts (qt)

Metric

1 liter (L) = 1,000 milliliter (mL)

Units of Weight (Customary)

1 pound = 16 ounces (oz)

1 ton (T) = 2,000 pounds (lb)

Units of Mass (Metric)

1gram = 1,000 milligrams (mg)

1 kilogram (kg) = 1,000 grams (g)

Sari's Cloth

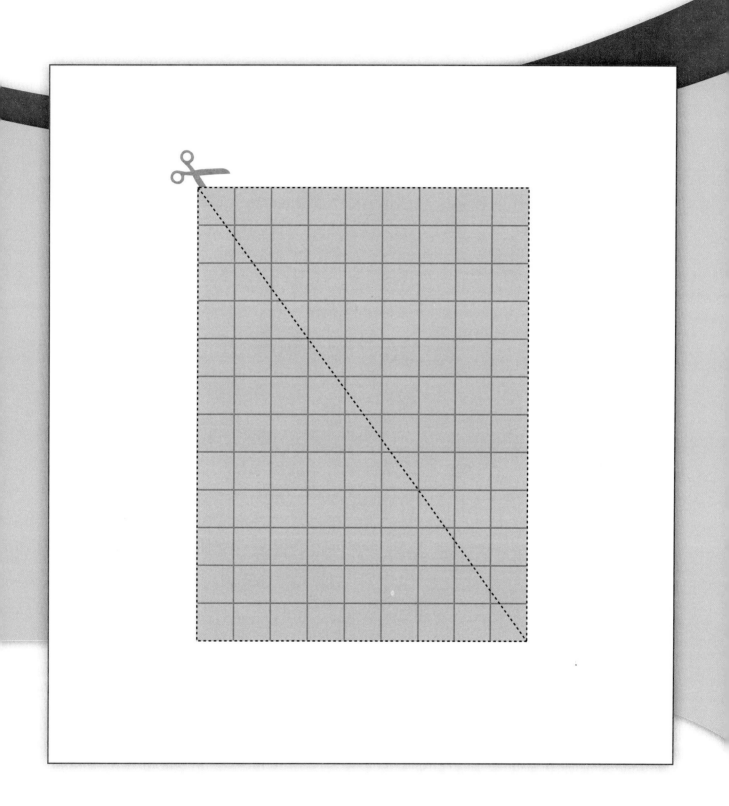

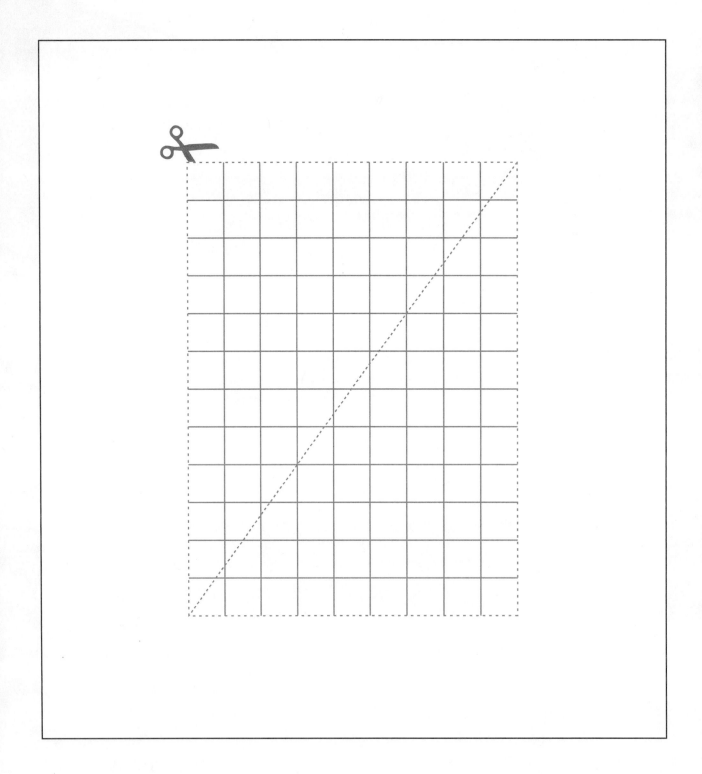

Solid Shape Patterns

Cut out both nets. Fold along the dotted lines and tape each solid together.

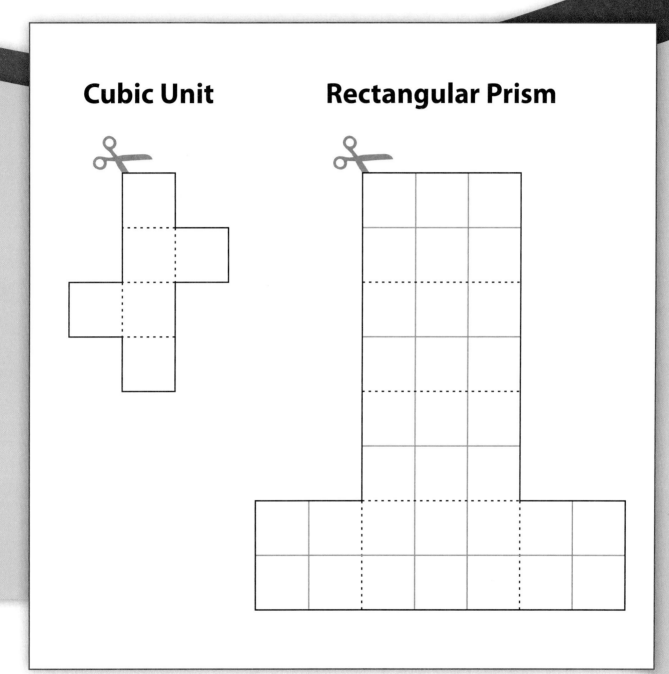

Cubic Unit

Rectangular Prism

Graph Matching Activity

Susan's Workout

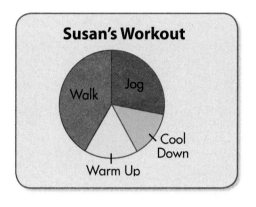

After-School Club Membership

Hobby Club	🧍 🧍 🧍
Chess Club	🧍 🧍 🧍 🧍
Art Club	🧍 🧍 🧍 🧍
Drama Club	🧍 🧍 🧍 🧍
Science Club	🧍 🧍 🧍 🧍 🧍
Sports Club	🧍 🧍 🧍 🧍 🧍 🧍
Math Club	🧍 🧍 🧍 🧍 🧍 🧍 🧍 🧍 🧍

Each 🧍 = 4 members

Favorite Sports

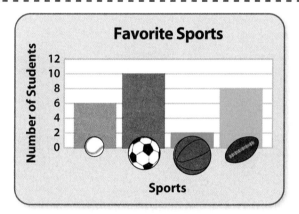

Growth of Greta's CD Collection

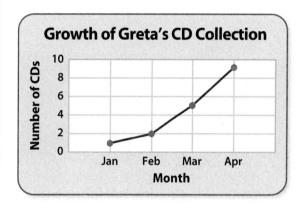

Age of Club Members

Age (in years)	Number of Members
9	1
10	2
11	6
12	7
13	2
14	3
15	1

Age of Club Members

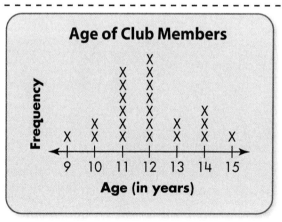

Display	Display
Display	Display
Display	Display

Graph Matching Activity

Picture Graph	**Line Plot**
Frequency Table	**Circle Graph**
Line Graph	**Bar Graph**

Term	Term
Term	Term
Term	Term